Ella in Hospital

Mary O'Keeffe

g **GILL** EDUCATION

On the calendar:

December
10th
Saturday

dog

Name the things in the picture that begin with d.

Look, trace and say

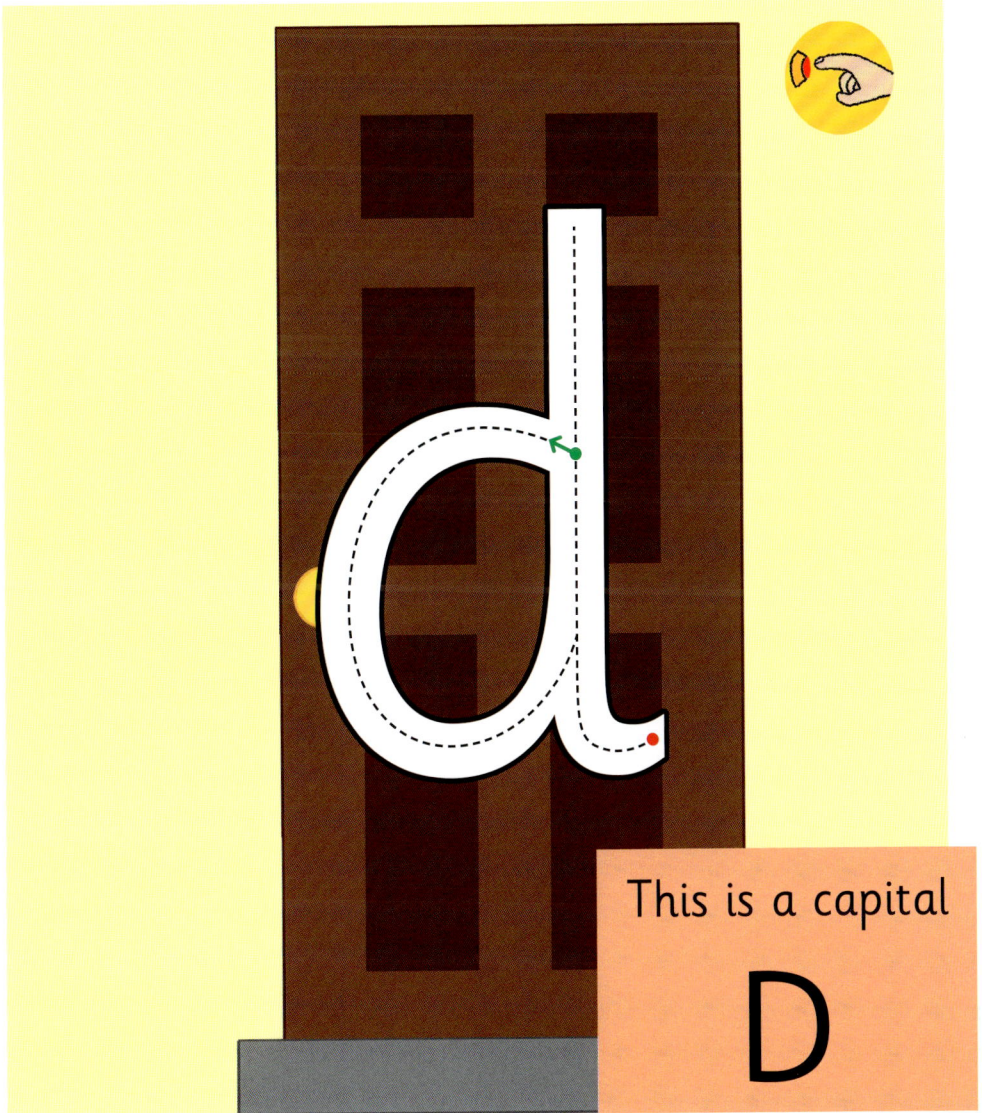

This is a capital

D

get

Name the things in the picture that begin with g.

Look, trace and say

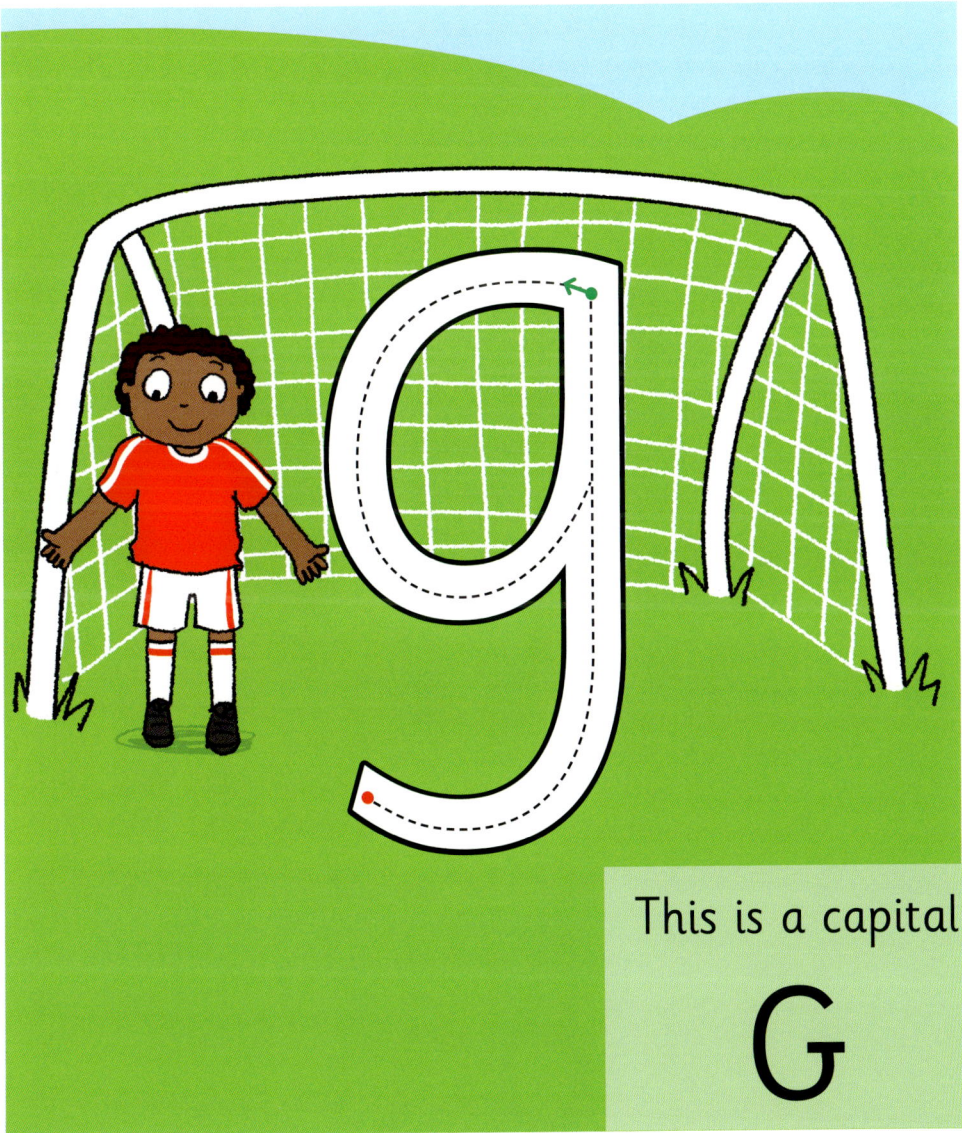

This is a capital

G

on

Name the things in the picture that begin with o.

Look, trace and say

This is a capital

O

Ella

UP → DOWN

up

8 Name the things in the picture that begin with u.

Look, trace and say

This is a capital

U

leg

Name the things in the picture that begin with l.

Look, trace and say

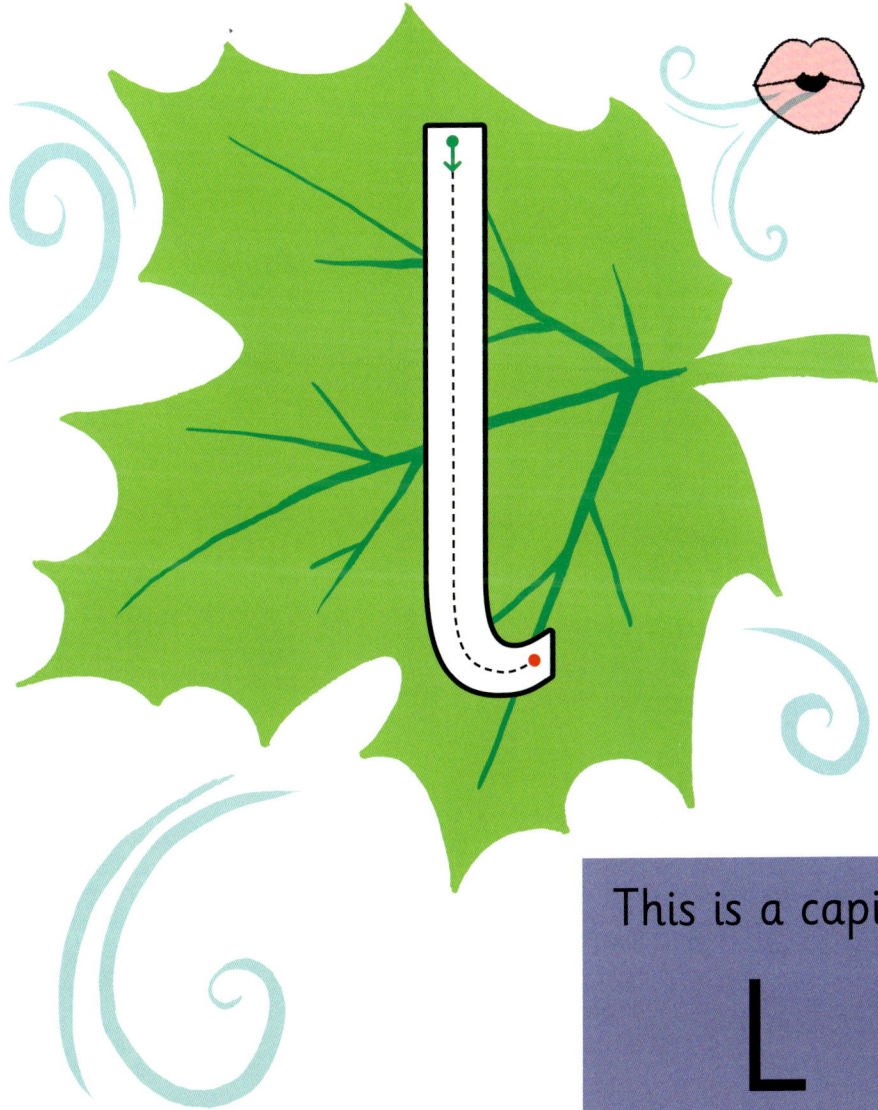

This is a capital

L

fit

Name the things in the picture that begin with f.

Look, trace and say

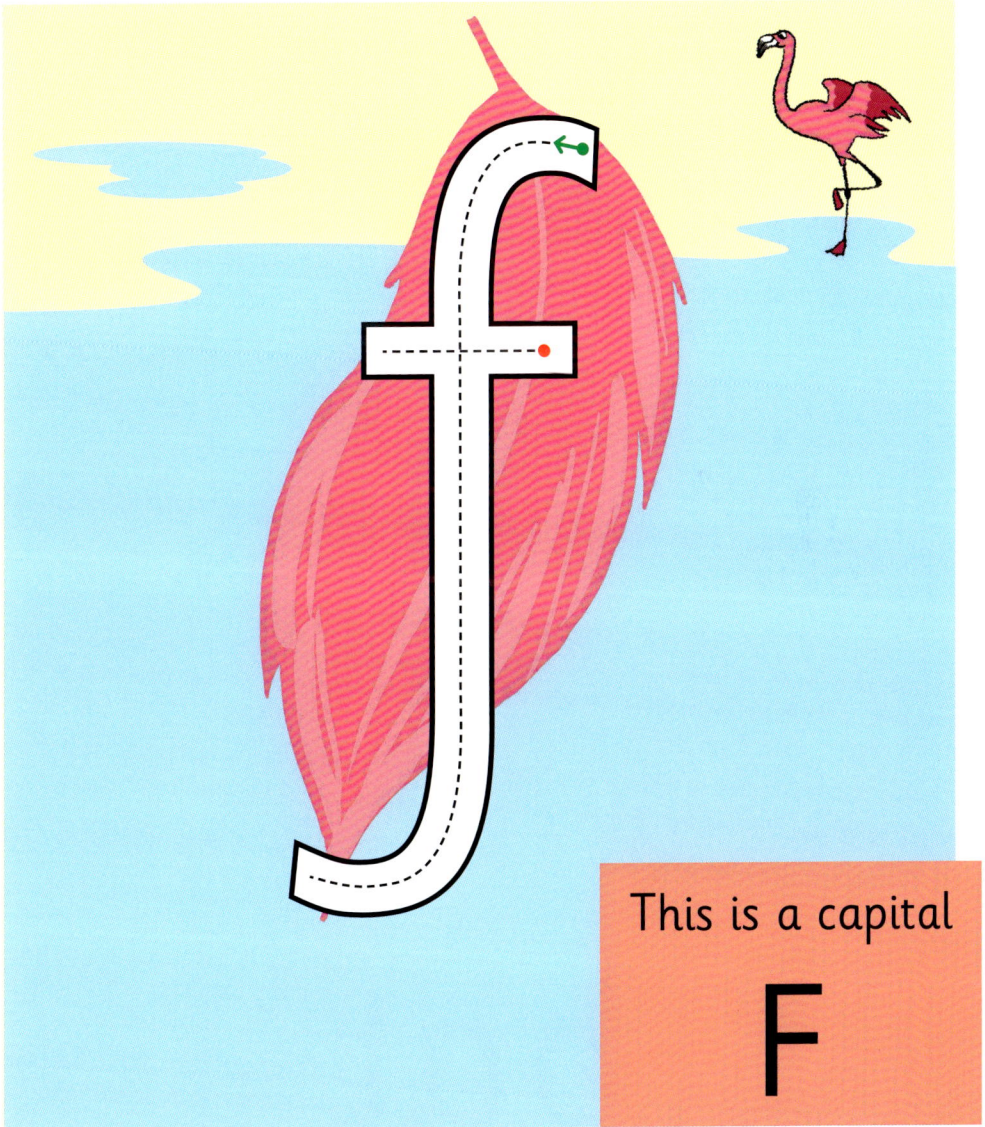

This is a capital

F

bat

Name the things in the picture that begin with b.

Look, trace and say

This is a capital

B

I can look, trace and say

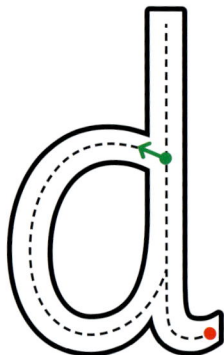

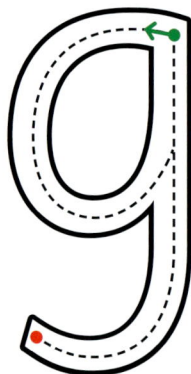

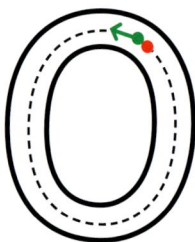

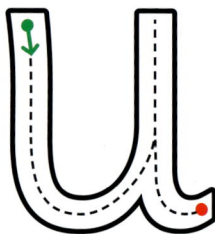

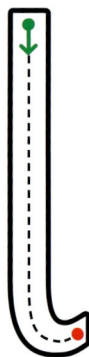

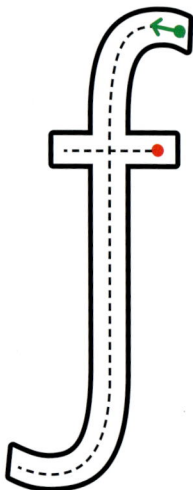

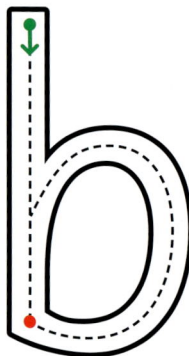

d g

o u l

f b